MYSTE OF THE PYRAMIDS

Written by Haydn Middleton

**Harcourt
Supplemental Publishers**

Rigby • Steck-Vaughn

www.steck-vaughn.com

Contents

Every year, people from all over the world visit some amazing buildings in Egypt. What are these buildings? They are the pyramids at Giza.

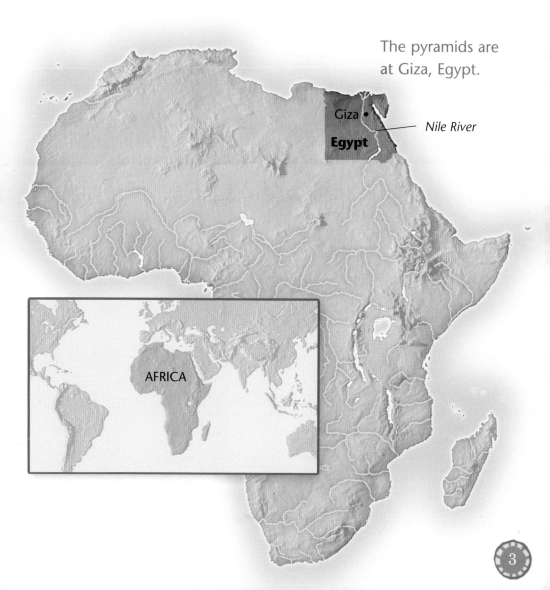

The pyramids are at Giza, Egypt.

Giza •

Egypt

Nile River

AFRICA

 So Many Mysteries

How and Why?

The Egyptians began to build the pyramids at Giza nearly 5,000 years ago. They built them with big blocks of stone. The biggest of the pyramids is called the Great Pyramid. It was once 481 feet tall. Now it is only 455 feet tall.

The pyramids of Egypt are full of mystery. How did the Egyptians build them? Why did they build them? For many years, no one could answer questions like these. Thanks to scientists, people now know the answers to some of the questions about the pyramids. But some of the answers are still mysteries.

For thousands of years, the Great Pyramid was the tallest building in the world.

How Were the Pyramids Built?

No one really knows how the pyramids at Giza were built. Scientists have looked at tools left near the pyramids to find the answer. They have looked for other clues, too.

Scientists think that thousands of people worked together to build each pyramid. They think that the people began by digging up stone. Then the people shaped the stone into blocks. Later, they put the blocks on top of each other like steps. When all the blocks were in place, the job was done. The pyramid was finished!

The pyramids were made from huge stone blocks.

The stone blocks used to build the pyramids are very heavy. How did the Egyptians lift the blocks? It's a mystery!

Today we use machines with motors to lift things. When the pyramids were built, the Egyptians had no machines with motors. Some scientists think the Egyptians dragged the blocks up ramps. But was there a better way to move the blocks? No one knows just what the Egyptians did to lift the heavy stone blocks.

Is this how the Egyptians moved the blocks?

Why Were the Pyramids Built?

Why did Egyptians of long ago build the pyramids at Giza? The answer to this important question rested deep inside the Great Pyramid for thousands of years. The doorway of the Great Pyramid was hard to see, so it kept the answer hidden. Four thousand years after the Great Pyramid was built, the first people found their way in.

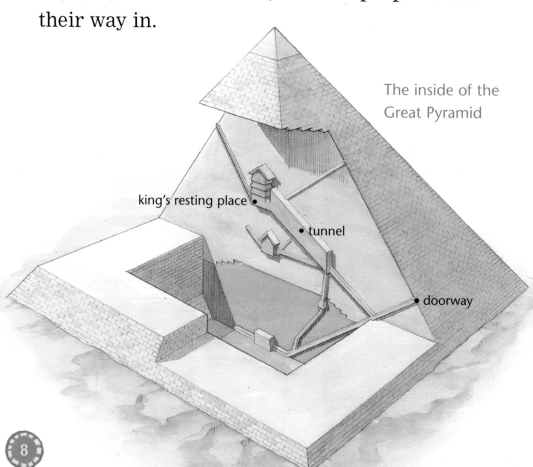

The inside of the Great Pyramid

king's resting place •

• tunnel

• doorway

Scientists believe a dead body once rested here in the Great Pyramid.

Inside the doorway of the Great Pyramid, a dark and spooky tunnel leads to a little room. There is no one in the room now. Some scientists think that 5,000 years ago, the Egyptians left a dead body there. Whom did they leave in the Great Pyramid? Some scientists think that the Great Pyramid was the final resting place for the king of Egypt.

Why Did Egyptians Choose the Pyramid Shape?

The sides of a pyramid are called faces. Each face has a triangle shape. Why did the Egyptians use this kind of building for resting places? It's still a mystery!

Faces of a pyramid at Giza

A painting of the Egyptian sun god Ra (at right)

Scientists know that the triangle sides of pyramids face north, south, east, and west. The front of each pyramid faces east. This is where the sun rises every day. The people of old Egypt believed there was a god of the sun. They called him Ra. Some scientists think that the Eygptians of long ago chose the pyramid shape to honor Ra.

Ra and the King of Egypt

The people of old Egypt believed their king was the son of Ra. They thought that Ra sailed a boat across the sky every day.

The Egyptians thought that Ra sailed across the sky in a boat.

Nearly 50 years ago, scientists found a pit near the Great Pyramid. The pit had 1,224 pieces of wood inside it. The scientists dug up all the pieces and fit them together. It took ten years to put the pieces together. When the scientists were done, the pieces made a big boat! Some scientists think the Egyptians made the boat for the king so that he could sail across the sky like they believed their sun god Ra could.

The boat found near the Great Pyramid

 Resting Places

Why Did Egyptians Make Mummies?

The pyramids were the final resting places for dead kings. The Egyptians dried the body of their dead king and wrapped it up. They turned the king's body into a mummy. Why did the Egyptians of long ago make mummies?

People in old Egypt wanted each king's body to last forever. They thought mummies lasted forever. They may have been right. Some mummies have lasted until today!

The mummies were really a mystery until about 200 years ago. That was when scientists began to look at mummies to try to figure out how they were made.

The mummy of this king of Egypt has never been found.

Mummies like this one are thousands of years old.

Why Did the Egyptians Make Other Resting Places?

The Egyptians made smaller resting places near the pyramids. Scientists think these places were for the bodies of people important to the king. The resting places had an upstairs and a downstairs. The dead body was downstairs. A statue of the dead person was upstairs.

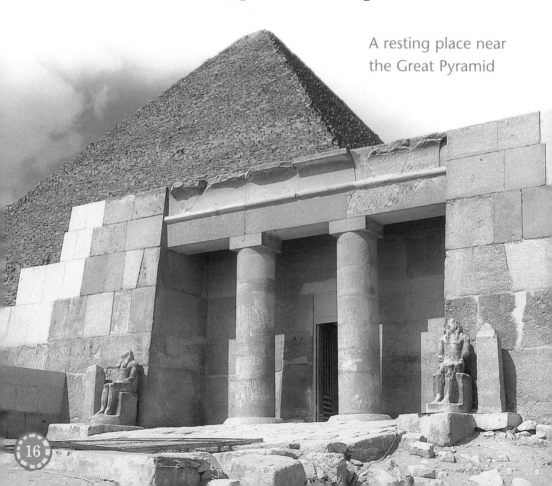

A resting place near the Great Pyramid

This dead person's statue is ready for gifts.

Scientists think that the room upstairs was for visitors to the resting place. Visitors left food, drink, and gifts there. Why did they do this? The Egyptians may have thought the dead person would need the things later!

Why Did Egyptians Write with Pictures?

The Egyptians wrote on the walls inside some pyramids. They sometimes wrote the names of the dead people. The writing looks strange to us. Egyptians of long ago didn't write with letters like we do. They wrote with little pictures!

It is hard to unlock the mystery of the old Egyptian writing. Sometimes it goes from side to side. Other times it goes from top to bottom. Even scientists do not know how to read all the mysterious Egyptian writing. Was writing with pictures better than writing with letters?

The Egyptians wrote with about 700 different pictures.

Chapter 4

The Great Sphinx

Why Did the Egyptians Make the Great Sphinx?

A stone statue stands in front of the pyramids at Giza. It looks really strange. It has a person's head and a lion's body. This statue is called the Great Sphinx. It was made from just one block of stone! It is ten times taller than a person.

Why did the Egyptians make the Great Sphinx? It's yet another mystery that scientists today are still trying to solve. Did the Egyptians want it to guard the pyramids? Was the Great Sphinx like a big guard dog? Can you think of a better idea?

Wind, water, and people have damaged the Great Sphinx over time.

The Dream of a King

A large flat stone stands between the two front legs of the Great Sphinx. The stone is carved with writing that tells the story of an Egyptian man. In the story, the man falls asleep near the Great Sphinx. The man dreams that the Great Sphinx asks him to dig it out of the sand that was all around. For the man's help, the Great Sphinx would make the man the king of Egypt. That man became king of Egypt in 1400 B.C.

The stone in front of the Great Sphinx is called a stele.

Many people visit the pyramids at Giza every year. Some of these people are scientists. They come to study these very old buildings. They come to learn more about the people of old Egypt, too. They also come to learn more about the pyramids and their mysteries.

Scientists are still trying to solve some mysteries of the pyramids.

Glossary

Egypt a country in the northeast part of Africa

Egyptian a person from Egypt

face a side of a figure

machine a tool that makes it easier to do hard work, such as lifting or moving something

mummy a dead body that has been wrapped and kept from decaying

scientist a person who studies and works in one area of science

sphinx a figure that has the body of a lion and the head of a man, hawk, or ram